THE CLASSIC RIDER WAITE SMITH TAROT

THE CLASSIC RIDER WAITE SMITH TAROT

A GUIDE TO USING YOUR DECK

Alice Ekrek and Tania Ahsan

Om Books International

Reprinted in 2026

Om Books International

Corporate & Editorial Office
A-12, Sector 64, Noida 201 301
Uttar Pradesh, India
Phone: +91 120 477 4100
Email: editorial@ombooks.com
Website: www.ombooksinternational.com

Sales Office
107, Ansari Road, Darya Ganj,
New Delhi 110 002, India
Phone: +91 11 4000 9000
Fax: +91 11 2327 8091
Email: sales@ombooks.com
Website: www.ombooks.com

ISBN: 978-93-6395-939-2

Printed in India

10 9 8 7 6 5 4 3 2

Contents

6
Introduction

9
History of the Tarot

11
How to Use the Cards

23
Tarot Spreads

49
Major Arcana

95
Minor Arcana
Wands 96
Cups 104
Swords 112
Pentacles 120

128
Index

INTRODUCTION

The tarot unlocks in the psyche messages from a vast mysterious universe, one that may in fact be psychologically located in one's own subconscious. Modern tarot readers do not ask for their palms to be crossed with silver while they pronounce the swift arrival of a tall, handsome stranger. They are as likely to advise you on how to approach forthcoming challenges as they are to prophesize about what is due to happen to you.

The tarot's universal symbols speak of a journey; it is the one we all embark upon at birth and it is our own personal heroic path through life. So, even if you are sceptical about the power of the tarot cards to predict the future, there is much to recommend them as a guide to discovering what concerns you have lying just under the surface of your consciousness.

Some of the imagery of the deck can be worrying – the figure of Death cutting down souls or people falling headlong from a blazing tower – however, this should be considered in the manner of a dream after you awake. You will not die (or at least not immediately after drawing a Death card) and you are unlikely to plummet from a high vantage point either. The Death in the card is one necessary for transformation and change to come about and the people falling from the Tower are losing their long-held, manmade beliefs represented by the tower in the picture.

As you do a reading, remember that your fate is not predetermined and outcomes will change as you change your attitude, behaviour and responses. A reading is a snapshot of what is coming in the next 6-12 months for you and it is rare that a reader will be able to accurately draw cards for any longer period of time than that.

HISTORY OF THE TAROT

The origins of the tarot are not known, but evidence suggests that the cards as we recognize them have been in existence since the fifteenth century. The first set of tarot cards we know of, the Visconti-Sforza pack, is Italian in origin; the second and more complete set is known as the Charles VI pack, named after the king of France at the time, although this deck may also have originated in Italy. The earliest evidence of playing cards in existence dates back to ninth-century China, so it may be that medieval tarot cards were based on these earlier playing cards.

Tarot cards are thought to have been used in card games known as *tarocchi*. The only firm evidence we have that they were used to divine the future dates from the eighteenth century, although there is fragmentary evidence to show they may have been used for this purpose much earlier.

The symbolic images on the tarot cards reflect the medieval and Renaissance European cultures from which they emerged. There were many multicultural influences in Renaissance Europe, including hermetic thought from ancient Egypt and Greece and other divination systems such as astrology and the kabbalah. All these belief systems would have had followers at the time and the images on the tarot reflect this. However, although the cards are clearly rooted in the ancient past, there is a timeless quality to the symbolism that speaks to people across cultures today and ensures their continued popularity.

HOW TO USE THE CARDS

THE CHOICE OF DECKS

Today there are hundreds of different tarot designs to choose from, many of which have a theme or specific purpose, such as answering questions about love and romantic relationships or catering to every interest, from pets to Arthurian legends. Given the wide range of choice, it can be difficult for the beginner to decide which type to select. Ideally we inherit our cards from a relative or friend, but many of us buy our own packs and let our instincts guide us.

The most popular deck used today is the Rider Waite Smith pack, which was created in 1909, and is included in this set. It was designed by artist Pamela Colman Smith according to the instructions of Arthur Edward Waite – an academic, freemason and prominent member of the Hermetic Order of the Golden Dawn (a group similar to a masonic order, but interested in magical and occult theory) – and produced by the Rider company. Originally called the Rider Waite pack (but amended to include Smith's contribution), it is now the standard deck and has been used as a template for numerous others. We will look in detail at the meaning of the cards in this popular deck later on. Each card has its own meaning, which is applied to the context of the question being asked as well as to the card's particular position in a spread.

When learning the tarot it is advisable to understand the meaning of the cards and then develop your own personal interpretation as you become more proficient. In this way, you develop your own intuitive system. In time, you may even want to create your own deck of tarot cards.

THE MINOR AND MAJOR ARCANA

The tarot deck is comprised of 78 cards, 56 of which are divided into four suits and known as the Minor Arcana. The remaining 22 are picture cards known as the Major Arcana. Arcana is a Latin word meaning 'secret', 'mystery' or 'mysterious' and refers to the mysteries the tarot helps us to uncover.

The Minor Arcana cards correspond with the suits in ordinary playing cards and with the four elements of fire, earth, air and water as well as representing other esoteric qualities (see Table of Correspondence on page 14).

The Major Arcana cards are not thought to correspond with playing cards. They are often numbered from 0-21, although the order varies slightly depending on the deck being used. They usually follow from the Fool card at 0 through to the World at 21.

THE SUITS

In a standard tarot deck, the Minor Arcana has four suits, each of which corresponds to a playing-cards suit – the wands or batons (clubs), cups or chalices (hearts), swords (spades) and pentacles or coins (diamonds). There are four sets of cards in each suit and they are numbered 1-10, with the ace as the first card. There are also court cards in each suit, although the tarot has an extra court card – the knight.

	PLAYING CARD SUIT	ELEMENT	SEASON	TIMING	QUALITIES
WANDS	clubs	fire	spring	days	action, creativity, energy, enterprise, intuition, hope, potential
CUPS	hearts	water	summer	months	love, relationships, happiness, harmony, sensitivity, emotion, fulfilment
SWORDS	spades	air	autumn	weeks	ideas, communication, conflict, struggle, separation, resolution, change
PENTACLES	diamonds	earth	winter	years	money, work, talent, reputation, achievement, stability, material realm

Table of correspondence of the Minor Arcana

THE COURT CARDS

There are sixteen court cards in the tarot pack; each of the four suits has a king, a queen, a knight and a page.

If a court card appears in a spread, it may represent an individual in your life who possesses the card's particular attributes. However, it can also represent qualities of the querent which need to find expression.

The kings represent mature male authority figures who embody power, paternalism, achievement and responsibility. Queens are mature, maternal females and, like the kings, figures of authority. They embody wisdom, confidence, fertility and life-giving qualities. Knights are immature men and women who are rash in their actions and tend to pursue their own desires and interests at the expense of others. Knights indicate change and movement in a new direction. Pages refer to children or young teenagers of either gender and represent youthful potential, dreams and other characteristics that are hard to define. The qualities they embody are delicate and need to be nurtured if they are to develop. Pages are messengers and indicate that news of some kind will be received.

ELEMENTS AND QUALITIES

The card suits also correspond to the four esoteric elements of earth, air, fire and water and their associated qualities (see Table of Correspondence opposite).

TIMING WITH TAROT CARDS

If a particular suit is dominant in a spread it may indicate when an event is likely to happen. The wands correspond with springtime and action, so represent the fastest unit of time (days); the cups correspond with summer and represent weeks; the swords correspond with autumn and represent months; and the pentacles correspond with winter and represent a year.

CARE OF THE CARDS

Everyone handles their cards in their own way, but part of the ritual and etiquette of using a tarot deck is to treat it with care. Practitioners are advised to keep the cards clean and wrapped in a cloth, pouch or placed in a box and stored in a private place when not in use.

It is advisable to become familiar with your cards and handle them regularly to build up a connection with them. In general, only the owner of the cards should handle them. In this way, you develop a deeper connection and when you come to consult the cards it is like approaching a personal confidante for advice. If you give a reading to another person (known as the querent), you may ask them to shuffle or cut the deck, but the querent's contact with the cards should be kept to a minimum.

PREPARING THE CARDS FOR A READING

Before the cards are laid out, they must be shuffled. It is worth focusing your mind on the question asked by the querent while you shuffle the cards. Then cut the deck once or three times and lay it out according to one of the spreads. Alternatively you can fan the deck out on a table and draw the number of cards required at random, placing each one in its position in the spread in the order you pick them. Some tarot readers leave the cards face down and turn each one over as they come to them during the reading.

Card readings can also be given using only the Major Arcana. The reader needs to separate these cards from the rest of the pack and shuffle them as normal.

GENERAL INDICATIONS

When many cards of the same suit turn up in a spread, it could show that a particular element or quality is influencing the matter. If Major Arcana cards predominate, it may suggest there are wider forces at work and that external factors will determine the matter. When mostly Minor Arcana cards appear, it may suggest that the matter is in the querent's hands. Aces represent new beginnings and, depending on their position in a spread, may indicate that the answer to a question is 'Yes'. The court cards may represent people in our lives who have the qualities ascribed to the cards, or they may direct our attention to those qualities in ourselves.

TIPS WHEN READING THE CARDS

The tarot is a complex system of divination. As with other forms of divination, on a superficial level it is just another form of fortune-telling. However, the cards have a deeper significance than mere prediction because they offer insights into the forces that are at work in your life and within your innermost self.

We should remember to approach the reading with humility, compassion and sensitive consideration for all involved – including ourselves, the querent and anyone else who crops up in the course of the reading.

The symbols should also be treated with care and used to help both reader and querent gain insights that will be of benefit. Whatever the nature of the cards selected, the reading should never end on a negative note. If the outcome is undesirable, we need to take the advice of the cards and consider how we can work towards a better outcome. Sometimes the cards may indicate that our desire for certain things will not lead to the best outcome for ourselves. It may take repeated readings, with the same results, before we understand and accept this message.

Sometimes the tarot can play up and will appear to give readings that don't seem relevant to the question posed. In these cases it is best to leave the cards for a while and start the reading afresh later on.

You have to work hard to get the most out of the tarot, but remember that words are no substitute for experience and being guided by others is no substitute for using your own instincts. Surrender to them and you will be richly rewarded.

REVERSED CARDS

When cards are reversed in a spread (drawn upside down), they can be interpreted as having the opposite meaning to the one they have when upright. However, some people only use the upright meanings of the cards and believe that a reversed card simply means that either something is blocking the outcome or that it will manifest more slowly. We will only use upright meanings here.

SELECTING A SIGNIFICATOR

A card can be selected to signify yourself, the querent and any other individual who may crop up in the reading. This card is called a significator, or signifier, and is usually the court card (page, knight, queen, king) which best describes the appearance and characteristics of the person in question.

The querent's astrological Sun sign may be taken into consideration when selecting the significator. For example, if the querent is female and her Sun is in an earth sign (Taurus, Virgo or Capricorn), then the Queen of Pentacles may be chosen to represent her – particularly if she also possesses the characteristics of that card, such as generosity, practical talents and a strong connection with nature and the physical world. If not, then another card may suit her better and this can be chosen as her significator instead.

The significator can be taken out of the deck and placed in the centre of a spread, or next to the spread, to set the tone and provide a focus for the reading. Alternatively, the significator can be left in the deck; if the querent's significator then appears in the spread, it can be understood to represent them in the reading or the qualities that they embody.

QUEEN OF PENTACLES

TAROT SPREADS

A single card may be selected from the deck to answer a question, provide general guidance on present events or serve as a focus for meditation. Alternatively, one of the spreads can be used to answer a question or give a general reading. There are many different ways to lay out the cards in preparation for a reading. Some of the more popular methods are listed here.

THE THREE-CARD SPREAD

One of the simplest layouts is the three-card spread. The first card is selected and placed face up – this represents the past. The second card is taken and placed on the right of the first card – this represents the present. The third card is placed to the right of the others – this represents the future.

SAMPLE READING USING THE THREE-CARD SPREAD

The querent is a young female in her early twenties. She has raised a question pertaining to a relationship that has failed. She is asking the cards to shed light on the situation and bring guidance to help her move on from the heartbreak and give an idea of what the future might hold.

The querent has selected the following cards:

1

2

3

Card 1: the past

This is represented by the Lovers card, which describes the experience of a deep connection with another person in the past. One might surmise that this was an important relationship that has had a strong effect on both people's lives. They may have felt they had made the right match. It would not be surprising if such a connection was difficult and painful to lose.

Card 2: the present

The Sun in this position suggests that the most important focus for the querent at present is herself and her own healing. Perhaps the relationship has awakened her self-confidence and creativity. She should concentrate on her creative potential right now and find joy and satisfaction through achieving her own goals and potential. In this way she will gradually heal the wounds of heartbreak and regain a connection with the self that may have been lost or compromised in a relationship with another.

Card 3: the future

The Hierophant in this position indicates that the experience of the relationship has led to a growth in wisdom and maturity. A new perspective on the matter will be found. A lesson will be learnt and will result in the development of a new personal philosophy and outlook on life. It may lead the querent to take a course of study or learn a new skill which will bring greater personal fulfilment.

Since all three cards are from the Major Arcana, we can surmise that greater forces are at work and the matter is out of the querent's hands. Perhaps the failed relationship was inevitable in some way – the two individuals were destined to meet, but the results of meeting and being forced to separate will lead to necessary changes in the querent's life.

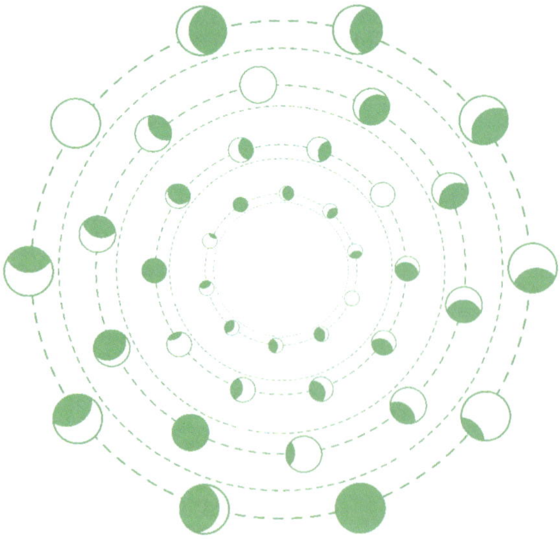

THE RELATIONSHIP SPREAD

This is a useful spread for interpreting your relationship to another person, be that your partner, your boss, a family member or friend. The cards for this example are laid out on page 28. Since it is a spread for the relationship between two people, make sure you keep the person in mind as you are shuffling and don't muddy the waters by thinking too much about the situation at hand. You may even find that what you thought was going on between you and the other person is the direct opposite, as in the case when someone is being aloof with you but secretly rather likes you.

1 What you think of the other person
2 What they think of you
3 The strengths in the relationship
4 The obstacles in the relationship
5 Where you are right now
6 What influences are likely to come into play
7 The final outcome

SAMPLE READING USING THE RELATIONSHIP SPREAD

A woman wishes to know where she stands with a long-standing on-off relationship with a man she knows.

1.What you think of the other person

The Emperor here indicates that she feels he can be a bit

1 The Emperor

2 Queen of Swords

3 The Devil

4 The Star

5 The Empress

6 Ace of Cups

7 Two of Swords

domineering and arrogant and attempts to railroad her into accepting elements of the relationship on his terms. This is not to say that she doesn't think well of him as the Emperor is a born leader and can be charismatic, charming and attractive.

2. What they think of you

Interestingly, the character of the Queen of Swords can be quite similar to that of the Emperor – she is analytical, strong and brutally honest. This card in this position does show that he is attracted to her humour and her integrity, but the problems may lie in how similar the two are to each other.

3. The strengths in the relationship

The Devil in this position shows a degree of eroticism in the relationship that is healthy and strong. The two are clearly attracted to each other physically and this aspect of the relationship is often what draws them back together.

4. The obstacles in the relationship

Alas there are too many hopes and expectations placed on the relationship, whether by the querent or the man she is asking about. This desire to have the relationship be what it isn't is blocking progress and frustrating each partner.

5. Where you are right now

The Empress card can often indicate a woman who is loved and content in that love, which is odd as the querent is clearly not content or secure in her relationship with this man. It could be that this is another woman in the man's life. It is also a card of fertility and may show an unexpected pregnancy.

6. What influences are likely to come into play

An Ace of Cups here reinforces the news of a baby. It is good here to check cards in the position before and after to see if it is a baby between the two people in the query or between one of the people and someone else. It seems likely here that the man has another relationship that will result in a child.

7. The final outcome

The Two of Swords is a card of self-defensiveness and of blindly fighting your corner. It seems as though this relationship is likely to hit some bumps and one of those might be a pregnancy one!

THE HORSESHOE SPREAD

In this spread, seven cards are laid out in a horseshoe shape. This spread is helpful if the querent has a particular question in mind or it can be used to give a general reading of current circumstances.

1 Three of Pentacles
2 King of Swords
3 The Empress
4 Six of Pentacles
5 The Hermit
6 The Hierophant
7 The Ace of Pentacles

The meanings of each card position are as follows:

1 The past

2 The present

3 Hidden influences

4 Obstacles that must be overcome

5 Others' perspectives

6 The best path to take

7 The final outcome

SAMPLE READING USING THE HORSESHOE SPREAD

A young man asked to have a general reading and selected the seven cards shown on page 31.

1. The past

The Three of Pentacles in this position indicates that the querent has been working hard and learning a trade of some kind. He has proven his skills and abilities to others and been recognized for his achievements in some way. Perhaps he has been trying to work out which direction to take with his career.

2. The present

The King of Swords in this position suggests that the querent is in a strong position of authority at this time. Perhaps his mental and analytical skills are being put to good use in his work as well as his private life. Or he may be in a particularly rational state of mind, able to think his options through and weigh them up to make the right decisions. He may be called upon to help others do the same. Being a court card, the King of Swords may also represent someone in the querent's life who displays these qualities and has an influence over the querent.

3. Hidden influences

The Empress in this position implies that a feminine figure has a hidden influence over the querent's life at the moment. Such a card may represent his mother or another female in his life. She is working for his benefit behind the scenes, trying to steer him in the right direction without his knowledge and only wants the best for him.

4. Obstacles that must be overcome

The Six of Pentacles in this position may indicate that the querent's wish to share his wealth with others is holding him back in some way. Perhaps he needs to be careful with his resources and save for his future.

5. Others' perspectives

The Hermit in this position suggests that others may be thinking the querent is difficult to reach at the moment. He seems to have retreated from his normal activities and relationships to take time to think about his life and where he is going. He doesn't seem to have much time for his loved ones and they are no doubt looking forward to hearing from him!

6. The best path to take

The Hierophant in this position suggests that the querent needs to work out what is meaningful and important to him. Perhaps he will seek advice from a wise counsellor who can help to steer him on the right path. The querent has many questions about his meaning and purpose in life and may need to take some time to get in touch with his thoughts.

7. The final outcome

The Ace of Pentacles signifies that the final outcome will be the start of new business projects and ventures. Perhaps the card points to the setting up of a new business or to a job offer that is just what the querent was looking for. The purchase of a home, a sense of security and material comforts may also be indicated.

There are a number of pentacles in the spread, suggesting that career and financial matters are uppermost among the querent's concerns at the moment. Equally, the high number of Major Arcana cards suggests that there is a higher purpose at work; the querent can therefore trust that his path will unfold as it should.

THE CELTIC CROSS SPREAD

The Celtic cross is one of the most widely used Tarot spreads today, covering general themes and providing a snapshot of a particular matter. In this spread, ten cards are laid out in the shape of a cross and a staff (see page 36).

The meanings of each card position are:

1 The querent (a significator card can be selected for the querent and used in this position or a card can be picked at random)

2 The obstacle or influences that have a bearing on the question

3 The question itself and the basis of the matter

4 The recent past - something that has just happened that has a direct influence on the question

5 The highest potential of the matter

6 The near future in relation to the question

7 Fears and concerns that the querent has about the matter

8 Other people's perspectives - how other people see the situation

9 The querent's hopes and wishes for the future outcome

10 The overall outcome of the matter

1 The Devil
2 Two of Wands
3 Seven of Pentacles
4 Ten of Pentacles
5 Page of Wands
6 Five of Cups
7 Six of Wands
8 The World
9 King of Wands
10 Six of Pentacles

SAMPLE READING USING THE CELTIC CROSS SPREAD

The querent is a man in his mid-thirties. He has asked whether he should buy a property, but is unsure if he should take on the responsibility of a mortgage at the moment.

1. The querent

A card was picked at random from the pack to represent the querent in the first position. The card selected was the Devil. This does not suggest that the querent is evil! It means that he has his own interests at heart and will put his needs first in this matter. It may indicate that finding shelter is a matter of urgency and the querent may find himself homeless unless the situation is resolved quickly.

2. The obstacle or influences that have a bearing on the question

The Two of Wands in this position suggests a lot of work and effort has gone into searching for the right home and that the querent has now stopped to take stock. Perhaps he finds himself unable to move forward to make the decision and close the deal.

3. The question itself and the basis of the matter

The Seven of Pentacles in this position reinforces the suggestion that the querent is tired and weary after a period of hard work and research into buying a home. This may be deterring him from going ahead with buying a property. He is advised to stop for a rest and take stock of the matter before moving forward.

4. The recent past – an event that has a direct influence on the question

The Ten of Pentacles in this position suggests that material wealth and stability have been achieved. Perhaps the querent has saved enough money or received an inheritance that makes it possible to purchase a property. A great store of personal resources is indicated by this card.

5. The highest potential of the matter

The Page of Wands in the position of the highest potential represents a creative spirit who calls for excitement and adventure. This card may represent the querent's own creative potential or it could be someone else who has influence in the matter. This card suggests that the querent's priority is not to get tied down in one place but to maintain a carefree lifestyle. For this reason, it does not look likely that the client will be purchasing the property at the moment.

6. The near future in relation to the question

The Five of Cups in this position suggests that the client's dreams and wishes may be dashed. Perhaps the opportunity to buy the property he has set his heart on will be lost and disappointment will follow. Or perhaps a relationship problem or breakup will affect his decision.

7. Fears and concerns the querent has about the matter

The Six of Wands in this position suggests that the querent is afraid of success! Everything he wants is within his grasp but this may be causing such anxiety that he is unable to move forward. The querent should consider why he fears the possibility of achieving everything he set out to do. This card, together with the placement of the fifth card, suggests that perhaps he is frightened of the responsibilities that come with success.

8. Other people's perspectives – how other people see the situation

The World in this position suggests that other people think the world is the querent's oyster! They may believe he is in the enviable position of being able to do whatever he pleases and that limitless opportunities are open to him. Other people's opinions may be encouraging him to act cautiously to ensure he is not squandering the opportunities available to him.

9. The querent's hopes and wishes for the future outcome

The King of Wands in this position suggests that the querent has high aspirations. He dreams of travelling and seeing the world before settling down. The querent should follow his intuition and take the path that helps him to realize his dreams and achieve his greatest potential.

10. The overall outcome of the matter

The Six of Pentacles in this position indicates that after achieving his dreams the client will be able to share his wealth and success with others. While his wealth may diminish slightly (it was the Ten of Pentacles in the past, now it has been reduced to the Six of Pentacles), he will find a way to use his resources for the benefit of all.

The majority of cards in this reading are wands, followed by pentacles, which means that freedom and discovery take priority over settling down into a stable routine. After the heartache that may be on its way in the near future (indicated by the sixth card placement), the querent will be free to pursue his dreams and should follow his intuition in making decisions about the future.

THE ASTROLOGICAL SPREAD

The astrological spread is based on the twelve houses of the Zodiac. It is laid out in the shape of a circular horoscope, with one card chosen to represent each of the twelve houses (see page 42). If we compare the horoscope to a clock face, the first card is laid at nine o'clock, the second at eight o'clock and so on, in an anti-clockwise direction, with the twelfth card at ten o'clock. This spread is often used to get a snapshot of the querent's life at the moment and can answer questions about various aspects, such as relationships and career.

The areas of life covered by each card position are as follows:

1 The querent's appearance and persona
2 Personal values and monetary matters
3 Communications and short journeys
4 Home and family
5 Romance, creativity and children
6 Work and health
7 Relationships and business partnerships
8 Shared resources, inheritance and secrets
9 Teaching, learning and long journeys
10 Vocation, career goals and aspirations
11 Friends, groups and community
12 Unconscious and hidden realm

1 Eight of Pentacles
2 Nine of Cups
3 Ace of Cups
4 Eight of Cups
5 Seven of Cups
6 The Emperor
7 Knight of Wands
8 Page of Pentacles
9 Five of Wands
10 Ace of Pentacles
11 Strength
12 Ace of Wands

SAMPLE READING USING THE ASTROLOGICAL SPREAD

The querent is a female in her early forties who would like a general reading about relationships and career matters. We can look to the fifth and seventh house positions in particular to describe relationships, and the second, sixth and tenth houses for an indication of career prospects, although all the cards have a bearing on the chart. We should also look at each house position to get a general picture of a person's current experiences.

The querent has selected the following cards:

1. The querent's appearance and persona

The Eight of Pentacles in this position suggests that the querent is working hard to achieve her goals and perhaps training and learning new skills. To others, she might seem consumed by work at the moment and very serious about her career.

2. Personal values and monetary matters

The Nine of Cups in this position indicates that great wealth and emotional security are possible. Work is extremely satisfying and rewarding. If this does not describe the querent's current job, it should do so in the near future if the querent continues on her current path.

3. Communications and short journeys

The Ace of Cups in this position describes the ability to communicate with others from the heart. A new friendship or romance may begin as the result of a chance meeting while on a short journey. A love letter may be on its way.

4. Home and family

The Eight of Cups in this position suggests that the querent needs some time away from her home and family to gain some perspective and learn to appreciate them again. It also indicates that it might be helpful for the querent to explore her family background and roots.

5. Romance, creativity and children

The Seven of Cups in this position points to the need to make a decision regarding a lover. If it is relevant, there may be a choice involving children. The querent may be feeling creative at this time and should listen to messages arising out of the imagination and dreams to help her come to a decision.

6. Work and health

The Emperor in this position suggests that a decision needs to be made about the querent's job. This could involve taking on increased responsibilities as well as the wider decision about what job the querent really wants to be doing. The Emperor card recommends self-discipline and suggests that a father figure may have influence over the querent's decisions. The querent should make sure she fulfils her responsibilities at work and maintains a good healthcare regime.

7. Relationships and business partnerships

The Knight of Wands in this position represents a current partner or person about to enter the querent's life, who is fiery, courageous and brash. Perhaps the querent has had an argument with her partner that has resulted in angry scenes and caused her to question the relationship. The card might also signify that the querent's love life is about to take a new direction.

8. Shared resources, inheritance and secrets

The Page of Pentacles in this position indicates that the querent is being sensible with money and in matters that have been entrusted to her. She may be relied upon to keep a secret. In this placement, the card also suggests the querent has inherited a sense of responsibility and strong work ethic from her parents.

9. Teaching, learning and long journeys

The Five of Wands in this position suggests a crisis in the querent's personal philosophies and beliefs. Perhaps the fiery arguments with her partner stem from this. The querent may need to visit a conflict zone or she may be met with hostility when travelling to a distant location. As indicated by the first card in the spread, she is currently working to develop a new skill but may encounter obstacles that impact on her learning. The problem needs to be addressed head on and a resolution found.

10. Vocation, career goals and aspirations

The Ace of Pentacles in this position represents great material rewards and achievements in the querent's career and chosen profession. Perhaps a new job opportunity or business venture is imminent. This placement indicates that the querent is on the right track to achieve her career goals and ambitions. Her hard work and diligence will pay off.

11. Friends, groups and community

The Strength card in this position shows that the querent is regarded highly by her friends and wider community. While she encounters conflict in other parts of her life, the querent is in a strong position to work for the benefit of those around her and may be asked to defend friends who are in need of assistance.

12. Unconscious and hidden realm

The Ace of Wands in this position is an interesting placement for such a lively and active card. It could suggest that the querent's intuition is particularly strong at this time and she should use it to navigate the way ahead. She may also need to explore her anger, which may be rumbling beneath the surface and could be a reason for the conflicts encountered in her relationships.

Overall, there are mostly cups and pentacles in this reading, reflecting the focus of the question which was on relationships (cups) and career matters (pentacles). It looks as though important decisions need to be made in both areas and that the querent has the diligence and commitment to succeed along whichever path she chooses.

THE MAJOR ARCANA

THE FOOL'S JOURNEY

0

The Fool

'I EMBARK ON MY JOURNEY WITH TRUST AND A LIGHT HEART FOR THE WORLD OPENS UP BEFORE ME...'

KEYWORDS

FRESH START

BEGINNING

FREEDOM

COURAGE

OPENNESS

TRUST

RISK-TAKING

The Fool is shown standing on the edge of a precipice, bag and rose in hand, with a dog at his heels. He is stepping into the unknown, alone except for his trusty dog, full of expectation and potential and unfettered by the doubts and cynicism that come with experience. The card suggests a choice must be made and a journey started into unknown territory. Courage is required to take the first step. The Fool is unaware of and unprepared for what awaits him, but through new experiences will discover his true potential.

I

The Magician

'I AM THE MASTER OF MY DESTINY AND HOLD ALL THE KEYS TO SUCCESS...'

KEYWORDS

SKILLS

POTENTIAL

MASTERY

RESOURCEFULNESS

WILL

POWER

CREATIVITY

ACTION

The Magician stands next to a table upon which lie a wand, a sword, a chalice and a pentacle. These represent the four Tarot suits and the four elements. Wand in hand, the Magician is about to use his powers to command his will. Above his head the infinity symbol, known as the cosmic lemniscate, represents the eternal and immortal force of energy. At this first stage of his journey, the Fool realizes that he has all the resources he needs to gain mastery over the material world of opposites and duality. The Magician is an authority figure who has the power to do good. Creativity and resourcefulness are needed to overcome obstacles.

2

The High Priestess

> 'I AM THE SEER WHO STANDS BETWEEN WORLDS AND MAKES MANIFEST THE UNMANIFEST...'

KEYWORDS

WISDOM

INTUITION

MYSTERY

SECRETS

HIDDEN KNOWLEDGE

UNSEEN INFLUENCES AT WORK

The High Priestess is also described as the veiled Isis. She is seated between two pillars which represent the great universal principles and mark the entrance to the sacred temple. She holds a scroll containing esoteric knowledge on her lap. On her forehead she wears the symbol of the phases of the Moon, representing the cycles of life and the creative force of the female. She stands for hidden knowledge, wisdom and intuition. When she appears in a spread it could indicate that some hidden forces are at work in a situation and one must look inward for the answer.

3

The Empress

'I AM THE LOVED AND CONTENT WOMAN, FULL IN HER POWER TO GIVE AND RECEIVE LOVE...'

KEYWORDS

ABUNDANCE

PLEASURE

CONTENTMENT

CREATIVITY

NATURE

NURTURE

BALANCE

FULLNESS

FERTILITY

RENEWAL

The Empress is Isis unveiled. Seated on her throne, she radiates the beauty that comes from harmony with nature. She is the great Earth Mother, in charge of the seasons, the fertility of the soil and production of the food which sustains us. At this stage of the journey, the Fool realizes that he needs to look after his health and physical needs.

The Empress indicates the possibility of marriage and motherhood as well as material gain. With careful attention and nurturing, a creative project will bear fruit. A situation is full of promise and has great potential.

4

The Emperor

'I AM THE RESPONSIBLE LEADER WHO ALWAYS KNOWS THE RIGHT ACTION TO TAKE...'

KEYWORDS

JUDGEMENT

DECISION

ACTION

RESPONSIBILITY

CHALLENGE

EFFECTIVENESS

SATISFACTION FROM ACHIEVEMENT

The Emperor is the card of fathering and indicates focus and the energy of accomplishment. The Emperor challenges the Fool to build something lasting to be proud of. The Fool is asked to make a decision about what he wants and what he values most in the world. He must then set out to achieve his goal. It will require hard work and unwavering determination and he will be judged on his abilities and the way in which he exercises responsibility. When this card is drawn, someone in a position of authority may offer advice that should be taken seriously.

5

The Hierophant

'I AM WISDOM IN ALL ITS FORMS; HEED ME AND PROSPER...'

KEYWORDS

LAW

TRADITION

RELIGION

MEANING

PHILOSOPHY

TEACHING

LEARNING

VISION

Also called the High Priest or Pope, the Hierophant is a wise teacher, priest or counsellor to whom we may turn at times of personal crisis. Like the High Priestess, the Hierophant is seated between two pillars at the entrance of the temple. However, unlike the High Priestess, the Hierophant represents the outer trappings and traditions of religious practice. At this stage in his journey the Fool must find meaning and seek answers to questions about the purpose of his life. This card indicates that we may be searching for meaning in life or we need to approach a situation with a philosophical outlook.

6

The Lovers

‘I WILL TAKE YOU TO THE PLACE OF CHOICE WHERE DECISIONS MUST BE MADE FOR GOOD OR ILL...’

KEYWORDS

LOVE

CONNECTION

SEXUAL ATTRACTION

UNION OF OPPOSITES

NEW POSSIBILITIES

TEMPTATION

CHOICE

In the card of The Lovers, we find a naked man and woman standing next to (and, in some versions, embracing) each other, with the man looking at the woman. The woman is looking up to the sky, where an angel is watching. The card alludes to the first lovers of the Old Testament – Adam and Eve in the Garden of Eden. Thus, along with love, relationship and the family, The Lovers card has come to represent temptation and the need to make a choice. At this stage of his journey, the Fool finds his match and decides to marry and unite the opposites within. The card suggests that a union is possible and there is hope for a bright future ahead.

7

The Chariot

'I AM THE CHARIOTEER WHO WILL GUIDE YOU TO YOUR GOAL...'

KEYWORDS

ACTION

CONTROL

FOCUS

STRENGTH

STABILITY

WILLPOWER

CONFLICT

STRUGGLE

CHANGE

TRIUMPH

The Chariot card represents gaining control over conflicting forces. The charioteer in the card is trying to control the two sphinxes which are pulling the chariot. The sphinxes – one black, one white – represent principles pulling in opposite directions. The opposites that were united in the previous Lovers card must now be kept moving in the same direction. At this stage in his journey, the Fool must use all his strength to keep on the right track. By seeing what has to be done and taking control of the situation, obstacles will be overcome. If we manage to keep the opposite forces on the same path, we will go far. Events are moving quickly.

8

Strength

'I AM THE COURAGE YOU DIDN'T KNOW YOU POSSESSED...'

KEYWORDS

STRENGTH

CONTROL

CONFIDENCE

BALANCE

INTEGRITY

COURAGE

GENEROSITY

COMPASSION

The card of Strength depicts a woman holding open (or forcing closed) the jaws of a lion, apparently without fear of danger. The lion represents our primal urges, the wild and ravenous beast within, yet the woman has succeeded in taming them. Like the Magician, she has an infinity symbol, or cosmic lemniscate, above her head, indicating that she has achieved a new level of consciousness and understanding. The Fool is gaining mastery over the primal forces that have governed him and his conscious ego is taking control. The card suggests that struggles may be ahead, but we have the courage and confidence to overcome any danger.

9

The Hermit

'I WALK THE SOLITARY PATH TO FIND MY WAY THROUGH TO ENLIGHTENMENT...'

KEYWORDS

SOLITUDE

WITHDRAWAL

DETACHMENT

CAUTION

PATIENCE

PRUDENCE

DISCRETION

LIMITATION

The Hermit stands alone on a mountaintop, holding up a lamp to light his way. He is wearing a cloak and carrying a staff to help him through the tough terrain. He has retreated from society to gain some perspective and look inward for answers. Through patient searching, he gains insight and connects with his intuitive knowledge. The Fool has reached maturity and questions his direction in life. When the Hermit appears in a spread, we may need to retreat from a situation so that we can recharge our batteries and have space to think. We are advised to work out what is important to us before taking any further action in a matter.

10

Wheel of Fortune

'I AM CONSTANTLY TURNING SO THAT WHICH IS LOW WILL RISE AGAIN AND THAT WHICH IS HIGH WILL FALL...'

KEYWORDS

LUCK

CHANCE

FORTUNE

DESTINY

CHANGE

SUCCESS

NEW DIRECTION

The Wheel of Fortune represents an unexpected element that will change the outcome of a matter. It may be good or bad, but generally indicates a turn of luck for the better and may herald opportunities and a new phase in life. Although we are responsible for shaping our own lives, this card suggests that luck and fortune may come along at any moment and change things for the better. When the Wheel of Fortune is drawn, an unexpected solution to a problem may present itself. Sometimes the card reminds us that 'what goes around comes around', and that past actions will be rewarded.

11

Justice

'I AM BALANCE THAT COMES WITH FAIR RECKONING...'

KEYWORDS

FAIRNESS

IMPARTIALITY

BALANCE

REFLECTION

DECISION

EQUALITY

TRUTH

Like the High Priestess and Hierophant, justice is seated between two pillars, suggesting a religious connection. Justice is one of the universal principles upon which society is built. The figure in the card holds a sword and points it upwards, indicating that justice will be upheld. The sword of justice is famously double-edged, however and a balance must be found between two opposing sides for there to be a fair outcome. Following the Wheel of Fortune card, Justice reminds us that we are accountable for our actions and urges us to be honest and fair. This card indicates that justice will prevail.

12

The Hanged Man

'I AM THE SACRIFICE WE MUST ALL MAKE TO ARRIVE AT THE TRUTH...'

KEYWORDS

PATIENCE

WAITING

SURRENDER

SACRIFICE

WISDOM

FORESIGHT

PLANNING

STRATEGY

EVENTUAL GAIN

The card of the Hanged Man depicts a man hanging upside down from a beam. His legs are crossed and he has reached an impasse. No further movement is possible for the time being. The card represents sacrifice and the willingness to face short-term losses to ensure long-term gains. The Fool must learn patience and how to act strategically to achieve the result he wants. An immediate advantage must be given up, but will eventually be replaced by a much better opportunity. All expectations should be surrendered for the time being.

13

Death

'I AM THE CHANGE THAT ALL MUST FACE IN ORDER TO BE BORN ANEW...'

KEYWORDS

ENDINGS

LOSS

MOURNING

ACCEPTANCE

ADJUSTMENT

CHANGE

TRANSITION

REBIRTH

RENEWAL

In the Rider-Waite-Smith deck, the card of Death is represented by a skeleton in armour riding a white horse over the corpse of a king. This suggests that the old order has ended and a new era is about to begin. At this stage in the journey, the Fool must accept approaching endings and uncertainty about the future. The endings may be difficult and painful, but we must learn to accept them. After a period of mourning and adjustment, we will be able to move on and embark on a new path. Change is inevitable. As we come to terms with loss, we are transformed.

14

Temperance

'I AM THE KEY TO
KEEPING YOUR HEAD...'

KEYWORDS

BALANCED TEMPERAMENT

HARMONY

MODERATION

COOPERATION

COMPROMISE

ADAPTABILITY

RELATIONSHIP

The Temperance card shows the figure of an angel pouring liquid from one vessel into another. This indicates that feelings are able to flow freely. It may signify a guardian angel watching over us. The card represents balance, healing and harmony. The Fool has learnt to master his thoughts and feelings and can now have harmonious relationships with others. We should act in moderation; compromise is the key to any problem. We have the ability to manage a situation and resolve problems. Events will run smoothly and success can be achieved. This card indicates that good relationships are possible.

15

The Devil

'I AM THE SHADOW YOU NEED TO SEE THE LIGHT...'

KEYWORDS

LUST

GREED

RAGE

PRIMAL INSTINCTS

SECRETS

THE SHADOW

SUCCESS IN CAREER AND PERSONAL INTERESTS

The Devil card may fill us with fear and dread because the Devil is a Christian symbol associated with evil. The card does not indicate evil, but asks us to confront the shadowy, instinctual part of ourselves. The Fool is reminded of those parts of himself that are self-serving and uncooperative, which he had tried to keep hidden away even from himself. When this card appears, things that we don't like to admit about our own character may be trying to break into our consciousness. A neglected part of us needs to be heard. It can also indicate success in career and you are advised to act in your own personal interests.

16

The Tower

'I AM THE CRISES THAT IS THE MAKING OF YOU...'

KEYWORDS

CONFLICT

OVERTHROW

DISRUPTION

DISAPPROVAL

UNEXPECTED CHANGE

The Tower card shows a tall building that has been struck by lightning. It is in flames and about to topple over. The lightning signifies that the gods are angry or disapproving. The Fool encounters sudden and disruptive changes and crises which force him to question his journey. This card suggests that the times are volatile, things are not going according to plan and the old order is in danger of being overthrown. We should not try to hold on and save the toppling tower; it is better to stand back and wait for things to settle. We may face uncertainty for a while. This card asks us to re-evaluate our current path. A sudden, complete change may be the best way forward.

17

The Star

'I AM HOPE, BRIGHT AS SIRIUS IN THE NIGHT SKY...'

KEYWORDS

HOPE

FAITH

MEANING

INSPIRATION

PROMISE

HEALING

PROTECTION

NEW HORIZON

The Star is a welcome symbol of hope, inspiration and rebirth to the Fool in the wake of the difficulties and uncertainties encountered in the Devil and Tower cards. In this card we see a star shining brightly in the sky above a beautiful woman who is emptying jugs of water into a stream. It represents feelings being returned to their source. Healing is possible and our sense of well-being is renewed. There is hope for the future and new possibilities are beginning to form. We are ready to give and receive love. The Star promises change for the better. This is a good time to meet new people, apply for jobs and aspire towards what is really important to us.

18

The Moon

'I AM THE FEAR THAT LURKS AT THE BOTTOM OF THE WATER...'

KEYWORDS

INTUITION

IMAGINATION

DREAMS

UNCONSCIOUS

FEARS

CONFUSION

DECEPTION

DISILLUSIONMENT

The Moon is associated with night, the unconscious realm and the dream world, where our deepest fears and imaginations run wild. The Fool has encountered a period of confusion and disillusionment. Where is the promise of the previous card and what does the journey hold next? Situations are vague and unclear; matters are not what they seem. We can act without being seen! We are advised to avoid deception and paranoia. At this time we can more easily tap into our unconscious and find creative solutions to problems. The way ahead is foggy, but we should allow our intuition to guide us.

19

The Sun

'I AM LIGHT AND WARMTH AND ALL GOOD THINGS TO ALL PEOPLE...'

KEYWORDS

JOY

OPTIMISM

CLARITY

TRUST

COURAGE

AMBITION

SUCCESS

OPPORTUNITY

HEALTH

VITALITY

HAPPINESS

The Sun, shown shining on a child riding a white horse, is symbolic of life in full bloom. The Fool has passed through his dark night and the way ahead is clear again. He knows where he is going and what he wants to achieve and he meets with success in all his endeavours. Indicating energy, joy, optimism and worldly success, this card suggests that it is the perfect moment to embrace opportunities and live life to the full. When this card appears in a spread, it promises health, happiness and perhaps even the birth of a baby.

Judgement

'I AM THE ONE WHO JUDGES THE WORTH OF THE ONE WHO COMES BEFORE ME...'

KEYWORDS

REWARD FOR PAST EFFORT

RE-EVALUATION

RESPONSIBILITY

OUTCOME

RESOLUTION

ACCEPTANCE

The Judgement card shows an angel, possibly Gabriel, sounding a trumpet above figures rising from their graves. It echoes the Day of Judgement referred to in the Bible, when Christ and his angels will return to Earth and even the dead will be judged on their deeds. This card can be understood to bring us the reward in life that we deserve. The Fool is forced to look at where he has come from, how he has behaved and the choices he has made. It marks a point at which we must re-evaluate our lives. We may need to learn hard lessons and be held responsible for past actions. We are advised to come to a resolution and move on with a clean slate.

21

The World

'I COMPLETE THE CYCLE THAT IT MAY TURN AGAIN AND BEGIN ANEW...'

KEYWORDS

INTEGRATION

FULFILMENT

ACHIEVEMENT

COMPLETION

ENDING

FINAL REWARD

SUCCESS

The World, represented by a dancing woman, is the final card in one complete cycle. The creatures at each corner of this card signify the four elements – fire (lion), earth (bull), air (eagle) and water (merman) – that form the fabric of our world. The Fool has accomplished much and learnt what he is capable of along the way. Challenges have been faced and battles fought and won. He is now ready to resume his position at the start of a new cycle. New challenges beckon and they can be approached with confidence. All things will be possible in the fullness of time.

THE MINOR ARCANA

DAY-TO-DAY LIFE, PEOPLE AND EXPERIENCES

Wands

Wands are associated with the element of fire and represent sparks of energy and the life force. They are represented by branches which are sprouting leaves, suggesting creation, regeneration and potential for the future. There is a great deal of energetic activity in the wands, which translates into action – sometimes creative and sometimes defensive or aggressive. Many wands in a spread indicate that events are moving quickly. Wands are sometimes referred to by other names, including rods, staves, staffs and batons, depending on which deck of cards or book you use.

'I AM FIRE AND SPEED.'

ACE OF WANDS

KEYWORDS: BEGINNING, CHANGE, OPPORTUNITY, ADVENTURE, CREATIVITY, HOPE, ACTION

The Ace of Wands signifies new beginnings and opportunities that can mark a change of direction in a person's life. There is the chance to embark on a journey or adventure, which may be sparked off by a new job opportunity, enterprise or relationship. The situation is full of hope and creative potential. It can also presage a birth in the family. Follow your intuition in taking up the right opportunities. Decide what you want to do and act quickly or you may miss your chance.

TWO OF WANDS

KEYWORDS: REST AFTER HARD WORK, PATIENCE, TRUST, PLANNING FOR THE FUTURE

The Two of Wands indicates that a new goal or project is on the horizon. It has taken courage, care and determination to formulate your plan, so now you can stand back and allow it to unfold and grow. Leaving the matter alone to allow the magic to work can lead to a period of restlessness. Patience and trust in the future are required. At this time you should make plans for the next stage and work out what to do once your creative endeavours have taken root and started to grow. Negotiations with others may be required. Travel may be indicated.

THREE OF WANDS

KEYWORDS: ACCOMPLISHMENT, SUCCESS, SATISFACTION, PROGRESSION

The Three of Wands represents hopes and plans that have been realized in the world. As the image on the card suggests, your ships are sailing home and success is on the horizon. The first stage of a project has been completed and there is a feeling of great satisfaction and pride in your accomplishment. But remember there is much work ahead so you must not become complacent. Avoid arrogance and remember you have not always been this fortunate and could lose your fortune again. The momentum of your success may propel you into the next stage of your project or creative endeavour.

FOUR OF WANDS

KEYWORDS: REWARD, BLESSING, CELEBRATION, HAPPINESS, HARMONY, ROMANCE

The Four of Wands suggests that you can reap the rewards of your achievements. The card promises a time of peace and harmony. It is a temporary calm before the storm – more hard work and energy will be required again soon to resolve problems and conflicts that will arise. But for the time being a great deal of satisfaction and celebration is in order.

Be charming and amiable and enjoy sharing your success with others. Romance may be in the air.

FIVE OF WANDS

KEYWORDS: FIGHTING, CONFLICT, OBSTACLES, COMPROMISE

The fives of each suit mark the crunch points along the journey. The Five of Wands suggests conflict, as demonstrated by the fight scene on the card. It can also indicate the possibility of lawsuits. In your effort to accomplish your goals you have had to make difficult decisions and possibly cut corners or stepped on other people's toes along the way. This may have been unavoidable, but now you must battle it out. Try not to compete, but find a way to resolve the matter; compromise, if necessary. You need to hammer out the problem and find a resolution. If you behave honourably, things could turn out to your advantage.

SIX OF WANDS

KEYWORDS: SUCCESS, LEADERSHIP, RESOLUTION, FORTUNE, ACCLAIM

In the Six of Wands, problems have been dealt with and a matter is on the point of being successfully resolved. You have the support of friends and colleagues in realizing your aims. Good news is on the way, so don't give up now. You should stay true to your original vision and goals. The card may indicate that you will receive public acclaim for your activities and efforts. Exams will have a positive outcome. Relationships are about to take a turn for the better.

SEVEN OF WANDS

KEYWORDS: UPPER HAND, POSITION OF ADVANTAGE, CHALLENGE, FORCE, REASSESSMENT

With the Seven of Wands you face another battle with others, but this time you have the upper hand. Remember to play fair, but maintain control over a situation and keep applying force. In the process you will learn to harness your competitive instincts to defend yourself and your creative endeavours. The challenges you face can also help you to reassess your plans and goals and modify your behaviour as required. This will make you stronger and more successful in the long run.

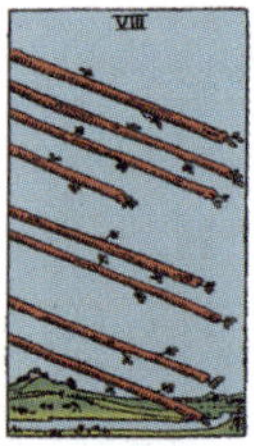

EIGHT OF WANDS

KEYWORDS: MOVEMENT, PROGRESS, BACK ON TRACK, GOALS ON THEIR WAY TO BEING ACHIEVED

The Eight of Wands represents a plan on its way to completion. You are back on track after a period of conflict and delay. Obstacles have been cleared and the way is free. You are focused on attaining your goals and forging ahead with your plans. Things are on the move. News may herald major changes in your life. Events are moving quickly and circumstances will soon change for the better. Things you hoped for will come to pass. Travel may be required to secure a matter in your favour.

NINE OF WANDS

KEYWORDS: FINAL CHALLENGE, GOAL IN SIGHT, PERSEVERANCE, TENACITY, DETERMINATION, COURAGE TO OVERCOME

The Nine of Wands represents last-minute challenges on your way to attaining a goal. You have come a long way and are determined not to give up now. Although it may not seem like it at the moment, what you have been hoping for is within reach. With your goal in sight, you find the courage and tenacity to give one final push. If you persevere, no obstacle can stand in your way for long. From deep within you must find the resources to keep going and remain hopeful.

TEN OF WANDS

KEYWORDS: ACHIEVEMENT, ATTAINMENT OF GOALS, SATISFACTION, EXPERIENCE GAINED, REST AND REGENERATION NEEDED

The Ten of Wands shows an old man reaching his final destination. He is hunched over with the weight of his load. You have come a long way and are weighed down with the responsibility of turning your vision into reality. Your efforts are about to pay off, but at a cost. You have been shaped by bitter experience and have lost the innocence and optimism of youth. As you reach the end of the cycle you can find satisfaction in all your achievements so far. You will need to rest and recharge your batteries so that new ideas can form.

PAGE OF WANDS

KEYWORDS: ACTIVE, PLAYFUL, IMAGINATIVE, INSPIRED, CREATIVE, YOUTHFUL, FOLLY

The Page of Wands is an active and boisterous youth with a fertile imagination. This card represents the urge to explore and play, to follow your dreams and look for new experiences and adventures. The Page seeks to avoid the responsibility that comes with maturity. When this card appears, it may represent a person, young or old, whose behaviour is eternally youthful. It may also represent your own need to break from stifling habits and responsibilities and develop these creative qualities within yourself.

KNIGHT OF WANDS

KEYWORDS: HONOURABLE, COURAGEOUS, HASTY, UNRELIABLE, AGGRESSIVE, VOLATILE, NEW DIRECTION

The Knight of Wands is a great warrior who loves to take risks and prove himself worthy. An honourable opponent, he defends the vulnerable and fights for their cause. He can be hot-headed and temperamental and may rush to conclusions. The card may describe someone you know who fits these characteristics or could indicate that you need to develop your warrior-like qualities to defend yourself or your loved ones. The Knight of Wands often signifies a move to a new home or a new direction in life.

QUEEN OF WANDS

KEYWORDS: STRONG, COURAGEOUS, GENEROUS, VIBRANT, CREATIVE, WISE, INTUITIVE

The Queen of Wands is a wise woman, independent and authoritative, imaginative and intuitive, strong and courageous. She knows what she wants and how to get it. The Queen makes a warm, lively host who is generous with her gifts. The card may describe a woman you know who fits these characteristics or may indicate that you need to develop these qualities yourself.

KING OF WANDS

KEYWORDS: INTUITIVE, DECISIVE, ACTIVE, INSPIRATIONAL, VISIONARY

The King of Wands is a mature man of vision who inspires others. He has strong leadership qualities and uses his wisdom and powers of intuition to guide him in decision-making. Sprightly and full of energy, the King engages with life to the full. The card could describe a man you know who fits these characteristics or indicate that you need to develop these qualities of leadership, activity and inspiration.

Cups

Cups are associated with the element of water and represent feelings, love, relationships and emotional fulfilment. They also signify the vast imaginative reserves within us and our unconscious realm. Water quenches our thirst and brings satisfaction and fulfilment.

'I AM WATER AND LOVE.'

The cups themselves are vessels for holding water and they are often full (indicating fulfilment); however, sometimes the water is spilt (indicating crisis and sorrow) or overflowing (suggesting abundance). Many cups in a spread signify that feelings and relationships are highlighted. The cups are sometimes referred to by other names, including chalices, goblets and cauldrons, depending on which deck of cards or book you use.

ACE OF CUPS

KEYWORDS: LOVE, JOY, HAPPINESS, ABUNDANCE, RELATIONSHIP, EMOTIONAL EXPRESSION, FERTILITY

The Ace of Cups, like the overflowing waters pictured on the card, indicates freely flowing emotions which need to find expression. There is potential for great emotional fulfilment. Deeply satisfying love and happiness are possible. The Ace of Cups represents the start of a new relationship or it can indicate a marriage proposal. There is the chance of a fresh start and a new lease of life. There is great hope for the future – your emotions will sustain you and love will find a way!

TWO OF CUPS

KEYWORDS: NEW RELATIONSHIP, ATTRACTION, ROMANCE, HARMONY, SATISFACTION, CONCEPTION, EMOTIONAL FULFILMENT

The Two of Cups heralds the start of a new relationship, romantic attraction or connection with another person. You have the capacity for deep satisfaction and fulfilment. It feels as though you have met your match in another person. You see yourself reflected and mirrored back by your partner and find out about new aspects of your character through his or her eyes. Existing relationships are strengthened. The card can indicate a marriage union or conception of a child or another creative endeavour.

THREE OF CUPS

KEYWORDS: PLEASURE, JOY, MARRIAGE, BIRTH, FEASTING, MERRIMENT, CELEBRATION, ABUNDANCE, FORTUNE

The Three of Cups indicates that there will be a happy gathering of people. This card may herald a pregnancy or marriage proposal or success in a creative endeavour close to your heart. You can be proud of your achievements. Joy and cause for celebration are indicated. This is a time to share your good fortune with others. You have renewed faith in the power of love.

FOUR OF CUPS

KEYWORDS: DISSATISFACTION, BOREDOM, DISCONTENT, DEPRESSION, CRISIS, RE-EVALUATION, SELF-QUESTIONING

In the image on the Four of Cups card a young man ignores the three cups he already has and the one being offered to him. For some reason you feel unhappy and discontented with your lot. You are in danger of developing a careless attitude towards life and becoming apathetic. You are entering a period of personal crisis and questioning and you have temporarily lost your connection with loved ones. You may feel that something is lost or missing from your life. The card indicates that you don't realize how fortunate you are. You need to take time to re-evaluate your life and decide what is really important to you.

FIVE OF CUPS

KEYWORDS: LOSS, SORROW, REGRET, DESPAIR, BETRAYAL, NEGLECT, EMOTIONAL BREAKDOWN, RELATIONSHIP BREAKUP

The Five of Cups can presage a relationship or marriage breakup. The image on the card shows a man in a black cloak turning his back and withdrawing from the world. Three cups have been spilled on the ground, indicating relationships that have been lost or thrown away. However, two full cups remain: this means you have a chance to hold on to whatever is left. You should think carefully before coming to a decision, for the effect could have consequences for yourself and your loved ones.

SIX OF CUPS

KEYWORDS: CALM, SERENITY, ACCEPTANCE, SIMPLE PLEASURES, NOSTALGIA, OLD FRIENDS, NEW HOPE AND OPPORTUNITY

The Six of Cups is the calm after an emotional storm. Although things might not be perfect, you learn to accept your limits and find a new appreciation of those close to you and with whom you share your life. Your thoughts may be focused on the past and you may start to idealize the 'good times' as you remember them. An old friend may re-enter your life and help you come to terms with what you have become, bringing a fresh opportunity and a new lease of life. New friendships can also blossom.

SEVEN OF CUPS

KEYWORDS: DECISION, CHOICE, DREAM, VISION, IMAGINATION, NEW PATH

The Seven of Cups suggests you are at a crossroads in life or in a particular matter. You have a very important decision to make and there appears to be more than one option open to you. In this card you see the cups situated in rows in the clouds. Each cup is filled with a different magical item. You may rely on the imagination, a dream or a vision to choose the right path. But you are advised to remain grounded and realistic when working with the imaginary realm or your decisions will be short-lived and you won't be able to stick with them for long.

EIGHT OF CUPS

KEYWORDS: RETREAT, ESCAPE, ABANDONMENT, LOSS, DISSATISFACTION, TIME OUT, PERSPECTIVE NEEDED

The Eight of Cups indicates that you may need to go away for a while to work out what is really important to you. You are unfulfilled and dissatisfied with your choices and find it difficult to choose something and stick with it. Nothing seems to bring the satisfaction for which you are yearning. You must find a way to gain some perspective on your life before deciding what to do next. The card can indicate that the time has come to move on. You may need to find a way to let something go and trust that things are on the right track.

NINE OF CUPS

KEYWORDS: WISHES FULFILLED, HOPES REALIZED, POSITIVE OUTCOME, CHILDBIRTH, JOY, SUCCESS, REWARD

The Nine of Cups is known as the 'nine months card' and indicates the birth of a baby or another creative endeavour. Something you have tended and nurtured has come to fruition. You are brimming with joy and the world is filled with hope again. Health and happiness are offered and the problems of the past have evaporated. A wish will be fulfilled and things will work out unexpectedly well. You can enjoy your good fortune and find satisfaction in what you have achieved.

TEN OF CUPS

KEYWORDS: LASTING HAPPINESS, JOY, FULFILMENT, EMOTIONAL STABILITY, FORTUNATE OUTCOME

The Ten of Cups is a card of emotional security and long-lasting fortune in matters of the heart. More happiness than you might have thought possible will be yours. The card indicates you have met, or will meet, the person with whom you want to spend the rest of your life. A situation has the best possible outcome. A stable, lasting relationship and family life are indicated. You can relax and enjoy the rewards of your efforts and good fortune.

PAGE OF CUPS

KEYWORDS: SENSITIVE, SYMPATHETIC, KIND, IMAGINATIVE, POETIC, LAZY, DAYDREAMER

The Page of Cups is a sensitive youth – a kind, generous soul who is easily hurt, feels other people's pain and is sympathetic to their needs. The Page may be naturally lazy at times and prone to daydreaming. He needs plenty of space to play and explore the imaginative realm. He or she may be oversensitive and may not take criticism well. News from a loved one could be indicated. This card may suggest a character who displays these qualities, or infer that these characteristics need to be developed within ourselves.

KNIGHT OF CUPS

KEYWORDS: ROMANTIC, CHIVALROUS, IDEALISTIC, QUESTING, HIGHLY PRINCIPLED, ON A MISSION

The Knight of Cups is the knight in shining armour of the pack, in all his romantic splendour. He rides around the kingdom searching for his love, ready to save her from any misfortune and ride off with her into the sunset. The Knight may also be on another quest – to seek the Holy Grail and restore the health of the King, bringing balance, peace and harmony to the kingdom. This card may describe a chivalrous young man or woman with a sense of mission and high ideals or it may highlight these characteristics within ourselves.

QUEEN OF CUPS

KEYWORDS: EMOTIONAL, SENSITIVE, CARING, PEACE-LOVING, HARMONIOUS, IMAGINATIVE, CREATIVE TALENTS

The Queen of Cups is in touch with her feelings. Wise and peace-loving, she is in tune with others. She is sensitive, sympathetic and kind-hearted. A good listener, she can advise others on matters that are causing concern. The Queen is a highly imaginative woman with creative gifts and talents. This card can represent a mature woman with these characteristics or it can refer to these qualities in your own character.

KING OF CUPS

KEYWORDS: KIND, HONOURABLE, RESPONSIBLE, RESPECTED, CONSIDERATE, EASILY SWAYED

The King of Cups is a kind, honourable male who is trusted and respected by others. He is naturally caring and puts the needs of his subjects first.

A just and fair ruler, he has earned the respect of others. He can be easily swayed and manipulated, however, so may become distrustful of others' motives. This card can be chosen to represent an individual with these qualities, or it may highlight these tendencies within ourselves.

Swords

'I AM AIR AND IDEAS.'

Swords are associated with the element of air and represent ideas, rational thought and communication. They concern the ideals of truth and justice. The swords are active principles and the cards describe circumstances in which you are called to fight for what you believe in. Their blades are notoriously double-edged, indicating that every decision you make or ideal you support may have both beneficial and harmful consequences. Swords are made of cold, hard metal, suggesting a lack of feeling or emotion. A number of swords in a spread indicates a focus on thinking – you may be called to fight for or be forced to reconsider your beliefs and ideals. Swords are sometimes referred to by other names, including daggers, knives and blades, depending on which deck of cards or book you use.

ACE OF SWORDS

KEYWORDS: BEGINNING, HOPE, IDEALS, PRINCIPLES, JUSTICE, CONQUEST, NEW DIRECTION

The Ace of Swords stands for your principles and ideals. You have decided to embark on a new life or take a new direction and have high expectations of your future. Justice will be done. You do not wish to compromise your strongly held beliefs. The card may indicate the birth of a child, bringing great hope for the future. You are asked to have faith in yourself and your ability to overcome any challenges that lie ahead.

TWO OF SWORDS

KEYWORDS: TENSION, BALANCE, STALEMATE, DIFFICULT DECISION, ACTION NEEDED

The Two of Swords indicates that a matter is in the balance and a difficult decision must be made. You cannot decide between two options open to you. The figure in the image on the card is blindfolded, suggesting that the way ahead is obscured. You must make a decision and stick by it. You should act now and not allow fears and doubts to hold you back. The sooner you make a decision, the sooner you can move on and find relief from a situation that is hanging over you.

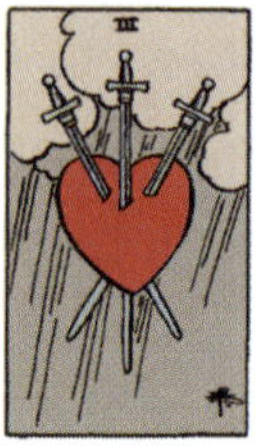

THREE OF SWORDS

KEYWORDS: CONFLICT, STRUGGLE, HEARTACHE, DISAPPOINTMENT, ARGUMENTS, TEARS, SEPARATION

The Three of Swords has the stark image of a heart with three swords passed through it. This card suggests the experience of pain and disappointment in matters of the heart, perhaps because of a love triangle. Feelings may be sacrificed in the interest of rational thinking. Quarrels and squabbles with loved ones are indicated. A separation of some kind may result. In gaining some distance from the matter you will find relief and realize that change was necessary in the long run.

FOUR OF SWORDS

KEYWORDS: REST, RETREAT, WITHDRAWAL, RECUPERATION, RELIEF FROM ANXIETIES, REBUILDING STRENGTH

The Four of Swords offers solace from a matter that has caused anguish. The card shows the tomb of a knight in a church; the effigy has his hands clasped in prayer. Something has been lost and part of you feels as though it has died with it. You need time alone to contemplate what has happened and where things might have gone wrong. You must rebuild your strength and reorganize your thoughts before you are ready to face the world again.

FIVE OF SWORDS

KEYWORDS: UNFAIR PLAY, DISHONOUR, BELLIGERENCE, LOSS, FACING CONSEQUENCES

The Five of Swords indicates unfair play and belligerent actions without consideration of their effects in the long run. You may have the upper hand in a matter, but your victory is double-edged and causes as much sorrow to you as it does to your adversaries. You have acted dishonourably and disobeyed authority to gain the upper hand. You must swallow your pride and approach a situation honestly and be prepared to face the consequences of your actions.

SIX OF SWORDS

KEYWORDS: SOLACE, RESPITE, RETREAT, HEALING, JOURNEY, INSIGHT, REPUTATION RESTORED

The Six of Swords may suggest that every ounce of strength has been sapped from you following a tough time, but the worst has now passed. The card indicates that a journey might be the best way to resolve a matter; this may be a journey in the literal sense or a journey of the mind. You are confronted with your subconscious thoughts and, as a result, insights may arise. You should allow things to sort themselves out without intervening. A matter that has been causing you great concern is on its way to being resolved.

SEVEN OF SWORDS

KEYWORDS: CUNNING, GUILE, DECEIT, TACT, DIPLOMACY, FLEXIBILITY, COMPROMISE FOR THE GREATER GOOD

The Seven of Swords indicates that a situation calls for you to behave falsely in order to attain positive results. The card shows a figure stealing swords from a military camp. While such an act may be dishonourable and your personal principles may be compromised, your actions may be necessary for the greater good. This card suggests there are times when your beliefs and ideals must be flexible and you should adapt them to the task at hand. Life throws many situations at us and we can't afford to be too rigid in our thinking when we come to deal with them.

EIGHT OF SWORDS

KEYWORDS: RESTRICTION, MISTRUST, INABILITY TO ACT, INDECISION, IMPRISONMENT, ISOLATION FROM OTHERS

The Eight of Swords represents restriction and mistrust. Like the Two of Swords, the figure in this card is blindfolded and afraid to act and face the consequences. The figure is also bound and surrounded by a wall of swords, as if held in a prison. A situation seems hopeless and you can't see a way out. You have run out of excuses and of ways to avoid making a decision – there is no escape. You must learn to trust others and should not be afraid to ask for help.

NINE OF SWORDS

KEYWORDS: FEAR, DOUBT, ANXIETY, NIGHTMARES, TROUBLED CONSCIENCE, SUFFERING, DESPAIR

The Nine of Swords represents great anxiety and suffering. The figure depicted on the card is in bed but unable to sleep; she holds her head in despair. Your hopes have been dashed, you are filled with fear and doubt and you struggle to come to terms with a matter. You blame yourself for an unfortunate outcome, but need to keep things in perspective. While it is necessary to face your part in a situation, you are only human and will make mistakes. You need to forgive and accept your limitations before you can lay the past to rest and move on.

TEN OF SWORDS

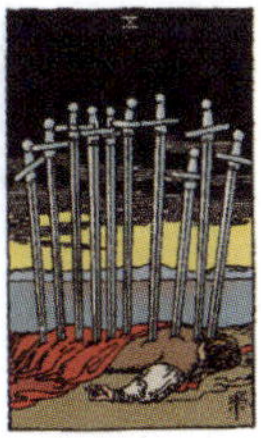

KEYWORDS: ENDINGS, MISFORTUNE, LOSS, DEFEAT, NEW UNDERSTANDING, FRESH PERSPECTIVE

The Ten of Swords represents defeat and marks the end of a difficult matter. The image on the card is of a man lying on the ground with ten swords in his back. At the end of a long struggle, something has been irrevocably lost. You must put the past behind you and move on to the next stage of the cycle. While you have been defeated on this occasion, lessons have been learned and you will move on with a new understanding of yourself and a fresh perspective.

PAGE OF SWORDS

KEYWORDS: CURIOSITY, INTELLIGENCE, WIT, HONESTY, INDEPENDENCE, CLASH WITH AUTHORITY

The Page of Swords is a clever, witty youth with a natural curiosity and inquisitive nature. He is in the process of developing his own ideas and beliefs and may frequently clash with authority over differences of opinion. The youth's independent ideas and curious spirit should be encouraged and nurtured rather than quashed. This card may represent a boy or girl who displays these qualities or may suggest that such gifts should be developed by the querent.

KNIGHT OF SWORDS

KEYWORDS: FIGHTER, WARRIOR, REFORMER, PREPARED TO MAKE SACRIFICES FOR JUST CAUSES

The Knight of Swords is a brave warrior who fights for the causes he believes in and is charged to protect. The Knight challenges injustice wherever he sees it and shows courage against all odds. He is willing to make sacrifices to uphold his principles and fights for justice, fairness and reform. Change will be brought about. This card may represent a young man or woman who displays these qualities or could suggest the time is right for the querent to develop such characteristics.

QUEEN OF SWORDS

KEYWORDS: JUST, FAIR, INTELLIGENT, FAITHFUL, WARRIOR, STRONG BELIEFS, IDEALISTIC, HIGHLY PRINCIPLED

The Queen of Swords has a strong mind and keen intelligence. With a cool exterior, she may sometimes seem icy or aloof, but she is always kind and fair toward her subjects. The Queen will argue her opinions with a clear head and keen insight. She is not afraid to fight for her principles if her duties require it. When this card is selected, it may represent a female who displays these qualities or may indicate the time is right for these characteristics to be developed by the querent.

KING OF SWORDS

KEYWORDS: INTELLIGENT, LOGICAL, FAIR, LAW-MAKER, JUDGE, COUNSELLOR, WARRIOR, STRATEGIST

The King of Swords is intelligent and known for his keen sense of logic and clear-headedness. He is an excellent judge and counsellor to his people and a capable warrior and military strategist. He has many innovative ideas, encourages reform and change and runs an orderly, civilized society. When this card is selected, it may represent a man who displays these qualities or could suggest that they should be developed by the querent.

Pentacles

'I AM EARTH AND ABUNDANCE.'

Pentacles are associated with the element of earth and represent matter, the body and the physical world. Pentacles are concerned with material security and finances as well as personal values and the sense of security that comes from within. This suit also represents physical health and well-being and the ability to draw comfort and satisfaction from personal possessions and the physical world. The pentacles themselves are in the shape of coins, suggesting money and earnings. Another word for money is talent; the pentacles represent talents and abilities that help us earn money and contribute to society in a useful way. Many pentacles in a spread suggest that material gain is highlighted in a matter and practical action may be required. The pentacles are sometimes referred to by other names, including coins and discs, depending on which deck of cards or book you use.

ACE OF PENTACLES

KEYWORDS: NEW VENTURE, OPPORTUNITY, PROMISE OF WEALTH, ACHIEVEMENT

The Ace of Pentacles suggests a new opportunity or venture that will put our innate talents to good use. Like the other aces, this card represents high hopes for success and an opportunity to make something of our talents, provided we use them wisely.

TWO OF PENTACLES

KEYWORDS: BALANCE, WEIGHING UP PROS AND CONS, CAREFUL CONSIDERATION, COMMON SENSE, RESPONSIBLE DECISION-MAKING

The Two of Pentacles is concerned with juggling or balancing two different duties, weighing up the pros and cons of a matter and making a carefully considered decision. In the image on the Rider-Waite-Smith deck, the figure balances two pentacles that are connected by the symbol of a cosmic lemniscate. This indicates that the figure must keep all his responsibilities in balance. If he fails to do so, he will be forced to drop one of the pentacles and the harmony between them will be destroyed. Behind the figure, ships sail on the ocean, but the rolling waves suggest that emotional imbalances affect your stability in the material realm. Under the circumstances, you are challenged to make the most practical choice you can.

THREE OF PENTACLES

KEYWORDS: CRAFTSPERSON, SKILLED ARTISAN, RECOGNITION OF ABILITIES, ACHIEVEMENT

The Three of Pentacles indicates that you will be recognized for your skills and achievements. Your handiwork is appreciated by others. You have worked hard and earned your success so far. While establishing a new venture you have honed your skills and built a good reputation. Now you must reassess your goals and develop in a new direction. You can start another project from a position of strength. Financial affairs will blossom.

FOUR OF PENTACLES

KEYWORDS: THRIFT, OVER-PROTECTIVENESS, LACK OF GENEROSITY, MISTRUST, PARANOIA, ISOLATION

The Four of Pentacles represents a withholding, ungenerous nature. You are afraid of losing what you have gained, so you hold on tightly to everything to prevent it being snatched away. You begin to become paranoid about other people's motives and are so afraid of losing what you have that you lose touch with others and become unapproachable. This card can indicate a tendency toward obsessive-compulsive behaviour, hypochondria and a fear of taking risks. It warns that self-imposed isolation and the desire for total control mean you are detached from the wider world and in danger of pushing away those who love you.

FIVE OF PENTACLES

KEYWORDS: FINANCIAL WORRIES, FEAR OF LOSS, DESTITUTION, FAILURE, SHAME, RE-EVALUATION, STARTING AGAIN

The Five of Pentacles indicates financial worries and fear of loss or failure. The image on the card shows two destitute figures outside a church, suggesting both material and spiritual impoverishment. The card may presage the failure of a venture, loss of a job or redundancy. You feel you have not lived up to your high standards and expectations. Your fear of loss may have led to this situation. You must reassess your behaviour and regain faith in your talents and abilities. You have the capacity to work hard, rebuild your reputation and achieve your ambitions.

SIX OF PENTACLES

KEYWORDS: SUCCESS, SHARING OF WEALTH, CHARITY, PHILANTHROPY, GIVING BACK TO SOCIETY

The Six of Pentacles signifies the sharing of good fortune with others. You have learned the lesson of the previous cards and now understand the consequence of holding on too tightly to material possessions. Plans are working out, you have succeeded in rebuilding your reputation in the world and can celebrate your success with others. Much satisfaction is gained from sharing time and money with worthy causes.

SEVEN OF PENTACLES

KEYWORDS: REST AFTER WORK, DISAPPOINTING RETURNS, RE-EVALUATION OF PROJECTS, REDIRECTING EFFORTS

The Seven of Pentacles indicates weariness after a period of hard work and suggests pausing to assess what you have achieved so far. It asks you to re-evaluate your plans and take stock of a situation. Are you on the best route to success? Perhaps you are overworked and disappointed with the rewards of your labours. A period of recuperation and regeneration may be necessary and you might want to take a short break if you can afford it. You should not lose faith, but pick yourself up again and implement the improvements that are needed.

EIGHT OF PENTACLES

KEYWORDS: NEW SKILLS, APPRENTICESHIP, CONFIDENCE, JOB SATISFACTION, REWARD

The Eight of Pentacles represents learning a new skill. You may be training in a new trade fairly late in life. You are slowly but surely gaining mastery in your work and can reap the rewards of your efforts so far. Financial gain and job satisfaction are indicated. Faith in your skills and confidence that you will achieve your ambitions will help you stay on the right path.

NINE OF PENTACLES

KEYWORDS: PLEASURE, SELF-ESTEEM, HUMILITY, SENSE OF ACHIEVEMENT, SATISFACTION, WINDFALL

The Nine of Pentacles indicates that you can take pleasure and satisfaction in your work and reap the rewards of your labours. You have worked hard to develop your talents and abilities and have proved yourself a capable and worthy member of society. You are realistic about your limitations and recognise that you have had failures along the way. However, you can be proud of everything you have achieved so far and can draw great satisfaction from recognizing where you have come from and what you have been through to get where you are today. An unexpected windfall might be indicated.

TEN OF PENTACLES

KEYWORDS: SECURITY, INHERITANCE, LASTING SUCCESS, SATISFACTION, SHARING, REWARDS, CONTENTMENT

The Ten of Pentacles indicates that lasting success and material satisfaction have been achieved. You have earned the right to relax and enjoy what has been accumulated through your efforts. The card suggests that you have also gained an inner sense of security. In addition to your personal wealth, a family inheritance may ensure that you live in comfort for a long time. Enjoying the company of your loved ones and sharing your fortune with them brings great pleasure.

PAGE OF PENTACLES

KEYWORDS: DILIGENT, RELIABLE, MATURE, LOYAL, STEADY, HARDWORKING, RESPONSIBLE

The Page of Pentacles is mature beyond his years and is the type of youth you can depend on – reliable and hardworking in his studies and keen to start working from an early age. The Page of Pentacles makes a loyal, steady friend. A message about money may be received. The Page may represent a youthful person who displays these qualities or may highlight the need to nurture these qualities in ourselves.

KNIGHT OF PENTACLES

KEYWORDS: SENSIBLE, CONSIDERATE, STABLE, RESPONSIBLE, RESPECTFUL, PRACTICAL, NERVOUS

The Knight of Pentacles is a practical, sensible, considerate character, with a strong sense of duty and respect for others. Unlike the other knights, the Knight of Pentacles acts with caution, taking care not to rock the boat. Knights are normally very active principles who fight for change of some sort. This knight needs to find a way of balancing these two tendencies or they will pull in different directions and lead to nervous tension. This card may represent a young man or woman known for these qualities, or may indicate the need to develop them in our own characters.

QUEEN OF PENTACLES

KEYWORDS: GENEROUS, STABLE, SENSIBLE, DOWN-TO-EARTH, WARM, COMFORTING, HEALTHY, CONTENTED

The Queen of Pentacles is practical, down-to-earth and generous with her gifts. She has an affinity with nature and animals and radiates comfort and confidence in her body. She enjoys tending to her surroundings and taking care of others. She can be relied upon to give fair, sensible advice and find practical solutions to problems. This card may represent a mature woman who displays these qualities or can highlight the need to develop them in ourselves.

KING OF PENTACLES

KEYWORDS: SENSIBLE, FAIR, HONEST, PATIENT, GENEROUS, PRACTICAL, TRADITIONAL, STABLE, HUMBLE, SELF-RELIANT

The King of Pentacles is an honest, generous leader who has worked hard and achieved great success. He upholds his duties and traditions and respects his ancestral heritage. The King finds practical solutions to problems and dislikes experimenting with new methods, preferring the old way of doing things. The King is kind, but has high expectations of others and expects them to have the same self-discipline and work ethic that he has. This card can represent a mature man who displays these qualities or can indicate the need to recognize them in ourselves.

INDEX

Chariot, the................. 64
Charles VI pack............ 9
Cups.................. 104-111
Death 76
Devil, the..................... 80
Emperor, the............... 58
Empress, the............... 56
Fool, the...................... 50
Hanged Man, the 74
Hermit, the.................. 68
Hierophant, the........... 60
High Priestess, the....... 54
History of the tarot 8
How to use the cards... 10
Judgement.................... 90
Justice 72
Lovers, the 62
Magician, the 52
Major Arcana......... 48-93
Minor Arcana 94-127
Moon, the 86
Pentacles 120-127
Spreads.................. 22-47
- Astrological..... 41-46
- Celtic cross...... 35-40
- Horseshoe 31-34
- Relationship 27-30
- Three card....... 24-26

Star, the 84
Strength....................... 66
Sun, the 88
Swords 112-119
Tarocchi 9
Temperance................. 78
Tower, the 82
Visconti-Sforza 9
Wands.................. 96-103
Wheel of Fortune 70
World, the 92